GRANT CAPTURED!

Lt. Gen. Ulysses S. Grant, Commander in Chief, Armies of the United States, a Prisoner of War

Walbrook D. Swank, Col. USAF Ret.

BURD STREET PRESS
SHIPPENSBURG, PENNSYLVANIA

Cover illustration, Major General Grant (Library of Congress).
Cover designed by Angela Guyer.

The acid-free paper used in this book meets the guidelines for permanence and durability of the Committee on Production Guidelines for Book Longevity of the Council on Library Resources.

For a complete list of available publications
please write
Burd Street Press
Division of White Mane Publishing Company, Inc.
P.O. Box 708
Shippensburg, PA 17257-0708 USA

Library of Congress Cataloging-in-Publication Data

Swank, Walbrook D. (Walbrook Davis)
Grant captured! : Lt. Gen. Ulysses S. Grant, commander in chief, Armies of the United States, a prisoner of war / Walbrook D. Swank.
p. cm.
ISBN-13: 978-1-57249-396-4 (pbk. : alk. paper)
ISBN-10: 1-57249-396-8 (pbk. : alk. paper)
1. Grant, Ulysses S. (Ulysses Simpson), 1822-1885—Imprisonment. 2. Imaginary histories. 3. Grant, Ulysses S. (Ulysses Simpson), 1822-1885--Headquarters--Virginia--Hopewell. 4. United States. Army--Supplies and stores--History--19th century. 5. City Point (Hopewell, Va.)--History, Military--19th century. 6. Hopewell (Va.)--History, Military--19th century. 7. United States--History--Civil War, 1861-1865--Campaigns. 8. Lee, Robert E. (Robert Edward), 1807-1870. 9. Confederate States of America. Army--History. 10. Confederate States of America--Politics and government. I. Title.
E672.S966 2007
973.7'3092--dc22

2007036205

PRINTED IN THE UNITED STATES OF AMERICA

Dedicated to

Harold Collier

and

Our Fellow

Civil War Historians

Other books by the author published by White Mane Publishing Co., Inc.

Old Abe's Jokes

Inside the Barracks

Courier for Lee and Jackson

Raw Pork and Hardtack

Battle of Trevilian Station

Confederate War Stories 1861–1865

Civil War Stories

Ballads of the North and South in the Civil War

Saddles, Sabres, and Spurs

Pacific Odyssey

My World War II Diary and the War Effort with War News Day by Day

Confederate Letters and Diaries, 1861–1865

Train Running for the Confederacy

Stonewall Jackson's Foot Cavalry

Defending the Southern Confederacy

Eyewitness to War in Virginia, 1861–1865

A Treasury of Confederate Heritage: A Panorama of Life in the South

Contents

Acknowledgments

Grateful acknowledgment and appreciation is due these publishers, authors, and institutions for making this work possible.

American Heritage Publishing Co., Inc.
New York, New York

Civil War, A Complete Photographic History
Black Dog & Levanthal Publishers, Inc.
New York, New York

Library of Congress
Washington, D.C.

National Archives
U.S. War Department, *The War of the Rebellion, 1880–1901*
Washington, D.C.

National Park Service
Petersburg National Battlefield
Petersburg, Virginia

Old City Point and Hopewell, The First 370 Years
By Mary M. Calos, Charlotte Esterling, and Ella Sue Rayburn
The Donning Company
Norfolk, Virginia

Sidelights and Lighter Sides of the War Between the States
By Ralph Green
Burd Street Press
Division of White Mane Publishing Co., Inc.
Shippensburg, Pennsylvania

Special credit and appreciation is given to these institutions for the photographs:

LC Library of Congress, Washington, D.C.

Virginia Tech Imagebase

Author's Note

This is the story of the activities of Lieutenant General Ulysses S. Grant, commander in chief, Armies of the United States at his headquarters at City Point, Virginia, where he established the most important and largest Civil War military supply base, and his fictitious capture by Confederate troopers.

Should the Confederate States government hold General Grant for ransom? If so, what would be the nature of that demand?

The author would like for the reader to suggest an alternative solution to the problem other than the one adopted by the Confederate States government as indicated in this narrative. You will receive a reply.

Send a suggestion to the author:

Colonel Walbrook D. Swank
C/o White Mane Publishing Co., Inc.
P.O. Box 708
Shippensburg, PA 17257
marketing@whitemane.com

Introduction

The capture of General Ulysses S. Grant would most likely be General Robert E. Lee's last great gamble. Over three years of a long, terrible war had left both sides with tremendous losses and a desire to end this conflict.

The Southern armies, although fighting valiantly and winning many contests, had become critically aware of the poor conditions within their ranks due to lack of supplies and insufficient replacements for the troops lost.

The armies of the North were also tired of the war, and the peace movement was growing. Perhaps if the delay caused by Grant's capture would embolden this political movement, the elections of 1864 would have a new president who would be willing to negotiate an end to the struggle. Many on both sides would welcome the end to the bloodshed.

General Lee had won many battles when the skill of his commanders and the troops they commanded had against all odds performed remarkably. General Grant always wanted to command from the field, and his seeming lack of concern and his willingness to be with the troops may just serve as the two major requirements to make a kidnap attempt possible and even probable. What could the South gain and what would the North lose if such an attempt were successful?

Part 1

The Road to City Point

The tide that swept the United States into the American Civil War had been churning beneath the surface for several decades. Erupting in 1861 with the Confederate capture of Fort Sumter in Charleston, South Carolina, the conflict grew quickly. In fact the day following the surrender, President Abraham Lincoln called for 75,000 volunteers for 90 days to put down the revolt. This action further divided the states with eleven states now officially seceded from the Union.

With Richmond becoming the capital of the Confederacy, the Union made the capture of this city the center of the war effort. With barely one hundred miles separating the two capitals, Virginia became a major area of conflict during the war. The first major conflict occurred at Manassas Junction on July 21, 1861, near Bull Run Creek. Thomas J. "Stonewall" Jackson earned his nickname at this battle and saved the day for the Confederacy by allowing time for reinforcements to arrive on the scene.

Assuming command of the Army of the Potomac after this defeat, Major General George B. McClellan made the first attempt to capture Richmond via the Yorktown Peninsula in March 1862. McClellan moved cautiously toward Richmond for several months and was to be joined by a force from the North under the command of General Irvin McDowell. To prevent this from occurring, Stonewall Jackson was ordered to threaten Washington, D.C., from the Shenandoah Valley. Jackson performed well and was then ordered to join the Army of Northern Virginia near Richmond.

General Joseph E. Johnston, the Confederate commander, was seriously wounded during the first day of what would become known as the Battle of Seven Pines and the Seven Days Battle. Assuming command, General Robert E. Lee brought as many troops as possible into his force and attempted to drive the Union army out of Virginia. McClellan, assuming his army was outnumbered, ordered a retreat.

Robert Edward Lee

Robert Edward Lee rose to become the general in chief of the Confederate States Army. A native son of Virginia, he was born at Stratford on January 19, 1807. His father, Henry Lee, was a Revolutionary War hero better known as "Light Horse Harry" Lee. Lee entered West Point in 1825 and graduated second in his class in 1829.

During the years before the Mexican War, Lee served in many assignments as an engineer in the United States Army. Assigned to the staff of General John E. Wool as captain, he was brevetted twice and was finally recommended to the rank of colonel after the battle of Chapultepec. Wounded during this battle he missed the final capture of Mexico City and the end of the war. Lee earned great praise from General Winfield Scott after the war when Scott stated that "Lee is the greatest military genius in America."

Lee returned to peace time duties as an engineer until he became superintendent of West Point from 1852 through 1855. Assigned to duty on the western frontier with the Second Cavalry, he would eventually command the department in 1860 and early 1861. During a visit to Washington in 1859 he was called upon by President James Buchanan to quell the John Brown raid on Harpers Ferry. Lee acted quickly, decisively forcing Brown to surrender.

March of 1861 brought Lee once again to Washington where General Scott offered Lee the command of the United States Army. Although opposed to secession, Lee would not serve in any invasion of the Southern states and resigned his commission to return to Virginia and accepted command of Virginia's forces on April 23, 1861. Seeing Lee's great organizational abilities, President Jefferson Davis used Lee as an advisor and designer of the defenses of the Southern states.

Robert E. Lee became commander of the Army of Northern Virginia when General Joseph E. Johnston was severely wounded during the battle of Seven Pines. Lee ably led the Army of Northern Virginia until the final surrender at Appomattox in April of 1865.

Lee, using this victory as a starting point, moved north to attack the newly created Union army under General John Pope near Manassas Junction in July of 1862. Outmaneuvering Pope, Lee destroyed the Federal supply base. Pope, deciding he could still win, attacked an entrenched Stonewall Jackson only to be outflanked by General James Longstreet and have his force decimated.

With another victory, Lee was now able to move further north and threaten the states of the Union with invasion.

The short-lived invasion of the North was brought to an end at the Battle of Antietam in September of 1862. This bloodiest day of the entire Civil War had over 23,000 casualties in only one day. Lee had gambled that he could split his forces only to have the orders lost and then found by the Union army. Working with the knowledge of Lee's plans, General George McClellan, once again the commander of the army, moved to destroy the Army of Northern Virginia. Only the heroic stand of the Southern army prevented disaster and helped Lee escape back into Virginia.

The year 1862 ended with the Battle of Fredericksburg. Here, once again, Lee showed his leadership and his engineering skills. Preparing positions on the heights overlooking the town, Lee lured General Ambrose Burnside, who had replaced McClellan, to attack the prepared positions. The slaughter of the Union army was inevitable, and this defeat led to the replacement of Burnside with yet another Union general, Joseph "Fighting Joe" Hooker.

May of 1863 found the Union army bogged down in the Wilderness near Chancellorsville,

Virginia. Lee and Jackson used this to their advantage and were able to attack the Union army in portions. Unable to use their superior numbers and weapons, the Union army was routed once again. Unfortunately for the Confederates, Stonewall Jackson was mortally wounded after the assault by his own men and would die from pneumonia a little over a week later.

Emboldened by this victory, Lee once again turned north to invade the states loyal to the Union. The people of both sides were growing weary of the war and would welcome an end to the suffering and violence. Perhaps bringing the war to the Northern homes would have the people demand just such an end. Crossing the Potomac River, Lee advanced up the Cumberland Valley into Pennsylvania. With parts of his army advancing on Harrisburg, York, and even threatening Baltimore, the people of the North were finally feeling the brunt of the war. Lee also used this time to gather supplies for his army from the rich farms of Pennsylvania.

Lee now divided his army into three corps. James Longstreet would command the First Corps, and Stonewall Jackson's old corps would be divided. General Richard S. Ewell would command the Second Corps and General Ambrose Powell Hill would command the Third Corps. Many consider the loss of Jackson as a great turning point in the war as Lee could always count on Jackson to deliver a victory using only very general plans for a campaign. Unfortunately for Lee and the Confederacy, Ewell and Hill would not operate as independently as Jackson had done.

The Battle of Gettysburg in July of 1863 marked the last great invasion of the North for the Army of Northern Virginia. On June 30, a division under the command of General Henry Heth entered Gettysburg to gather supplies, most notably shoes for his troops. On July 1 when Heth entered the town, he was confronted by Union cavalry under the command of General John Buford. The Union troops delayed the Confederate advance, and both sides brought reinforcements to the engagement. Lee arrived on the scene later that afternoon, and assessing the situation, decided the time was right to attack and so ordered Jubal Early's division into the attack.

That evening both sides settled into their positions, with General George Gordon Meade, the new commander of the Army of the Potomac, and Robert E. Lee both on the field guiding their men. Assessing the outcome of the first day's fighting,

Lee decided that he would launch an attack from the right using Longstreet's corps to attack near a peach orchard and a wheat field in an attempt to flank the Union left. Though successful with this attack, the Confederates could not carry the initiative into capturing Little Round Top and thus became stalled.

Lee, determined to make this invasion of the North successful, decided to attack the Union center on the third day of the battle in what would forever be known as "Pickett's Charge." Of the 12,000 men making the charge that day fewer than 50 percent would return across the field. With the losses that day, Lee finally decided it was time to return to Virginia. The Southern armies would never again invade the North in these numbers.

While the Battle of Gettysburg was being fought in the East, on July 4, General Ulysses S. Grant was capturing the important last stronghold on the Mississippi—Vicksburg. The Union army would now control the river and divide the Confederacy into two parts. Lincoln then placed Grant in command of the entire department of the Mississippi by combining the departments of the Ohio, Cumberland, and Tennessee. Grant's first action was to relieve the beleaguered Union troops in Chattanooga in October of 1863.

The year 1864 brought the changes that would eventually lead to the final campaigns of the war. Grant was promoted to lieutenant general in March and on the 12th was made general in chief of all of the Union armies. Grant placed General William T. Sherman in charge of the armies in the West, and Grant accompanied George Meade's Army of the Potomac in the East.

In May of 1864, Grant started the attack south toward Richmond. Fighting over the next few months would be over many of the same Virginia fields and towns as during the first years of the war. The difference was that Grant did not retreat even though he was "beaten" by Lee's army various times. Accepting the losses and continuing to press the Confederate army made the end seem almost inevitable. Grant kept trying to flank Lee or get between Lee and Richmond. Lee for his part continued to block the path and tried to lose as few men as possible. Grant finally crossed the James River and attacked Richmond from the south via Petersburg.

The plans to capture General Grant would be a last great gamble as the Confederate army was left no room to maneuver. The siege would only end if the political will of the North to wage the war could be broken, or if the loss of the head of the army would slow progress, and as a last chance, a possible exchange of troops for the return of Grant would allow the Confederate armies to gain much-needed reinforcements.

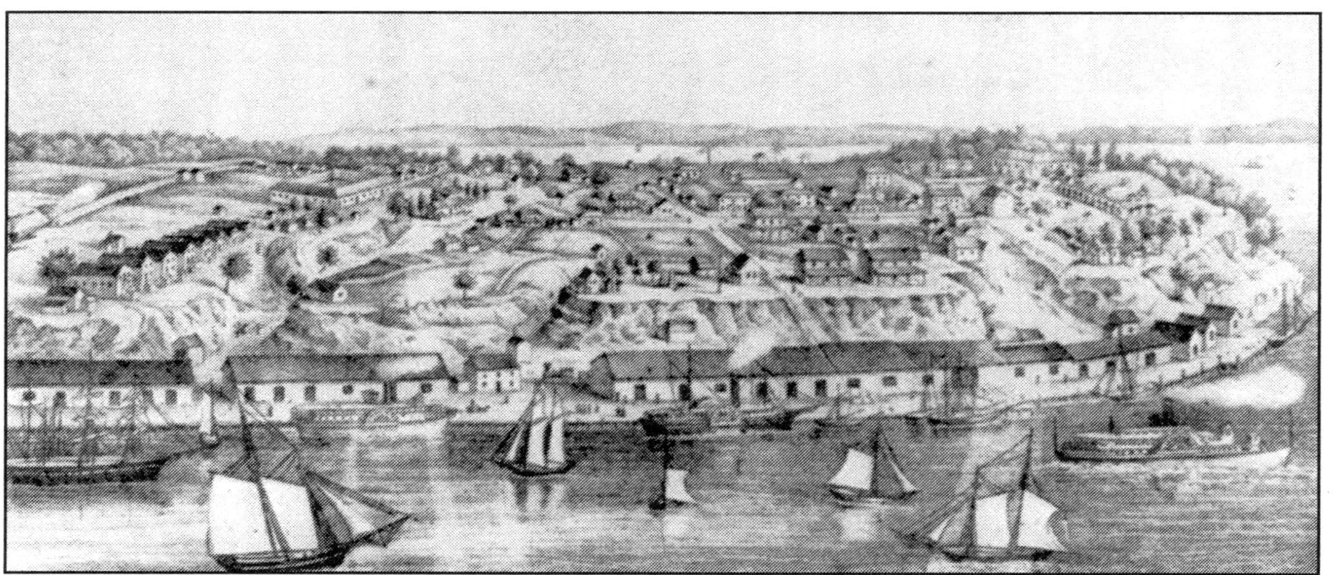

City Point at the confluence of the Appomattox with the James River, headquarters of the armies operating against Richmond.

LC

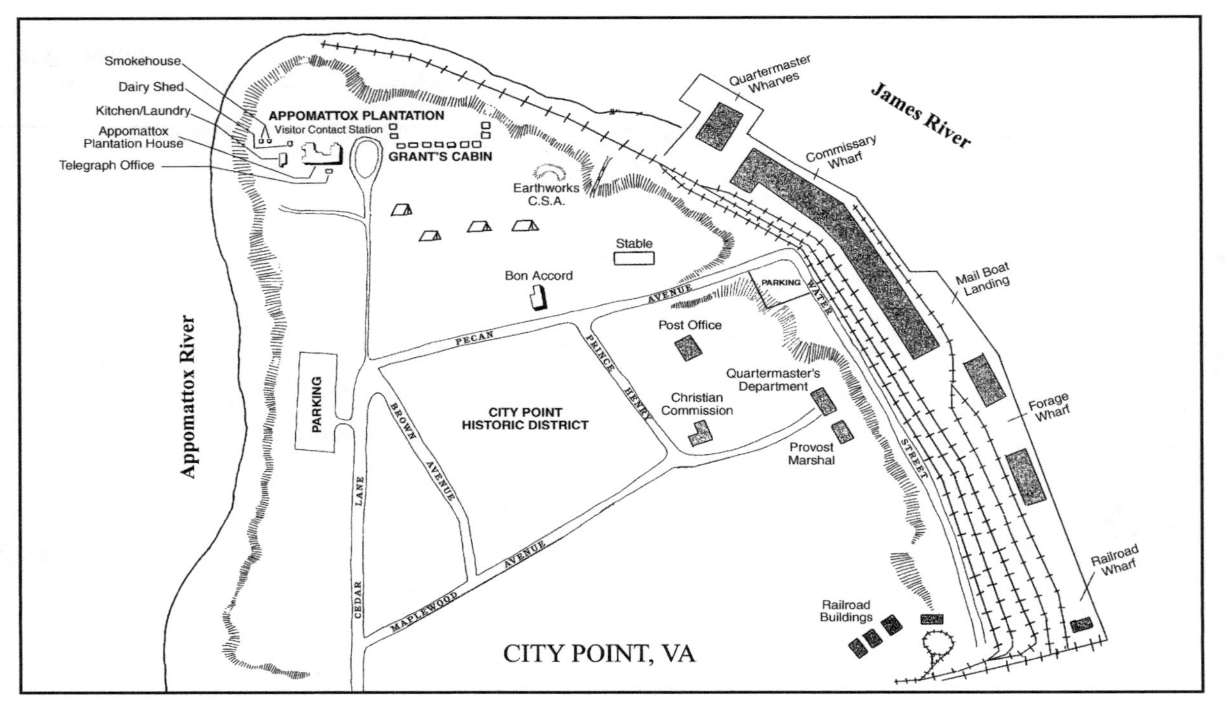
Smokehouse
Dairy Shed
Kitchen/Laundry
Appomattox Plantation House
Telegraph Office
APPOMATTOX PLANTATION
Visitor Contact Station
GRANT'S CABIN
Earthworks C.S.A.
Stable
Bon Accord
Quartermaster Wharves
James River
Commissary Wharf
Mail Boat Landing
Forage Wharf
Railroad Wharf
PARKING
WATER
STREET
AVENUE
PECAN
PRINCE
HENRY
Post Office
Quartermaster's Department
Christian Commission
Provost Marshal
Appomattox River
PARKING
CITY POINT HISTORIC DISTRICT
BROWN
AVENUE
LANE
CEDAR
MAPLEWOOD
AVENUE
Railroad Buildings
CITY POINT, VA

Part 2

City Point, Virginia, 1861–1865

Very few people, other than Civil War historians, are aware of the historical significance of City Point. In this narrative, we will try to correct that by bringing to your attention the prominence of this place in the era of the War Between the States.

The hamlet's population was made up mostly of fishermen and tradesmen. Dr. Richard Eppes was the largest landowner with about 2,300 acres, and his plantation home, Appomattox Manor, was over one hundred years old when war broke out. Dr. Eppes had about 130 slaves and was one of the richest men in the country. When his state seceded, he joined the Prince George Cavalry and served in the Third Virginia Cavalry. He bought uniforms for some of the men in his unit. Later, he left the company and became a contract surgeon in hospitals in City Point and Petersburg.

Early in the war, Southern troops served in the area, but in May 1862 a skirmish took place between the troops and Federal naval forces under control of Major General George B. McClellan's troop movement toward Petersburg and Richmond.

Confederate pickets captured four Union naval officers and five seamen. Three were killed and two wounded. The Union ships bombarded the area around City Point and Eppes's home, Appomattox Manor.

In May 1864, elements of Meade's Army of the Potomac and Major General Benjamin Butler's Army of the James landed at City Point and areas toward the Confederate forces near Petersburg. Brigadier General Edward W. Hink's Union troops of the XVIII Corps occupied City Point and attacked Petersburg on June 15, 1864, which started a ten-month siege of that city.

On the same day Lieutenant General Ulysses S. Grant, the new commander in chief of the Armies of the United States, established his headquarters on the ground around Appomattox Manor. He commanded seventeen military districts and over

Ulysses S. Grant

Ulysses S. Grant, the commander of the entire Union army in 1864, had a very unlikely rise to power after many unsuccessful endeavors. Born Hiram Ulysses Grant in 1822 in Ohio, he adopted the name Ulysses S. Grant when his appointment to West Point was filed incorrectly. When Grant arrived at West Point and discovered the wrong name, he tried to correct the error to no avail.

After graduating in the middle of his class, Grant saw service in the Mexican War. Because of his drinking habits as a captain in the army he resigned in 1854 and returned to his family in Missouri. There he had a rough time and peddled firewood on the streets of St. Louis. Forced to rely on the charity of his father, he moved to Galena, Illinois, and worked unsuccessfully in a variety of jobs until the war brought him back in uniform. At the outbreak of the Civil War he was appointed by the governor to command a volunteer regiment. In 1862, he successfully captured Forts Henry and Donelson where he earned the nickname "Unconditional Surrender Grant" after his terms for surrender of the forts: "no terms except an unconditional and immediate surrender can be accepted."

Grant's campaign to capture Vicksburg was the catalyst that brought him to be appointed the general in chief of the Union armies. It was in this role that he took the field with Gordon Meade's Army of the Potomac. City Point became the major supply base for the drive to Richmond and the destruction of Robert E. Lee's Army of Northern Virginia.

half a million men. Here he commanded the total war effort and set up the strategy for the siege of Petersburg. First from his tent and then from his cabin overlooking the confluence of the Appomattox and James Rivers, he directed operations and coordinated troop movements of Union armies in various areas of the country. Many notable governmental and military officials came to see him at his headquarters, including President Abraham Lincoln, General William T. Sherman, Admiral David Porter, and a Confederate peace commission including Confederate States Vice President Alexander Stephens. Grant's wife, Julia, and his son, Jesse, stayed with him in his cabin for the last three months of the siege of Petersburg.

Meanwhile, Dr. Eppes's wife and children stayed in Petersburg but moved to Pennsylvania during the siege and returned to Appomattox Manor with Dr. Eppes in 1865.

Facilities at City Point were greatly expanded after Grant's arrival. Almost overnight the little village became one of the busiest ports in the world as hundreds of ships arrived off its shores bringing food, clothing, ammunition and other supplies for the United States Army. On a daily basis, forty steamers, twenty-five sailing ships, and over one hundred barges delivered goods that were unloaded at a half-mile long wharf constructed for Union forces along the base of the bluff by a workforce made up mostly of African Americans.

Warehouses built along the waterfront allowed the quartermasters to stockpile vast amounts of supplies. On an average day during the siege of Petersburg, the Union army had stored around City Point food supplies for thirty days and enough forage for twenty days or nine thousand meals of food and twelve thousand tons of hay and oats for nearly one hundred thousand soldiers and sixty-five thousand horses and mules. The army also produced one hundred thousand rations of bread a day in bakeries it had built. The bread and other supplies were sent to the troops at the front by train and by wagon.

Using the old City Point railroad, the U.S. Military Construction Corps rebuilt the line west to

Petersburg, and then extended it southwest to the rear of Union lines. The twenty-six locomotives and two hundred railroad cars were brought by barge from Washington, D.C., to provide rolling stock for the line. In twenty-two days the army had completed the first stage of the railroad and had the trains operating on a full schedule. Along this twenty-one mile long rail line supply depots were built, field hospitals established, and communications systems erected. Over this rail line troops were transported to the front and the wounded were taken directly to the hospitals at City Point.

The Depot Field Hospital was the largest of seven hospitals operated at City Point and covered an area of seven hundred acres. The hospital, with a capacity of ten thousand patients, treated both Union and Confederate wounded, with a separate facility for black Union soldiers. The twelve hundred tents, supplemented in winter by ninety log barracks, comprised the compound that included laundries, dispensaries, regular and special kitchens, dining halls, offices, and other structures. Army surgeons administered the hospital aided by civilian agencies such as the U.S. Sanitary and U.S. Christian Commissions. Male nurses filled the army's ranks. A few women served as nurses and kitchen managers, and nearly two hundred black laborers kept the hospital clean and comfortable. Each patient had his own bed and washbasin and regularly received fresh pillows and linens. Covered walkways between the tents shaded patients from the sun, while water pumped up from the Appomattox River was used for cleaning and bathing. The excellence of the facilities and the efficiency of the staff and their dedication made the Depot Field Hospital not only the largest operation of its kind in the Civil War but also the finest and most efficient.

Soldiers remained at City Point for some time after the surrender at Appomattox Court House. Several thousand Confederate troops captured during the retreat were held at City Point waiting to be transported to prisoner of war camps. City Point had over 280 buildings plus a great number of winter huts and shacks built by the army. Even though former residents began returning shortly after the cessation of hostilities, life remained unsettled while City Point continued as a military base in the newly established First Military District.

In the era of Reconstruction right after the war, the South was divided into military districts and Dr. Eppes found his reclaimed house in Military

District #1. During this time the Eppes family boarded U.S. troops in their home, obtained government lumber and property, and dealt with some "rowdy" soldiers. Dr. Eppes helped teachers to instruct black children and provided a plot of land for a chapel to be built by the local African American congregation.

On September 1, 1865, Dr. Eppes stated in his diary that his plantation was "desolation personified, a perfect waste, not a house, fence, timber tree or scarcely tree of any kind standing everywhere more than 500 acres of woodland cut down." The grounds around his house contained forty-two cabins, and the shrubbery, fruit trees and garden had been nearly destroyed. When Eppes and other farmers returned to their fields, laborers had to be hired. Farmers along the James River agreed that monthly hands would be paid five to fifteen dollars a month, depending on job duties and skill of the laborer. Day hands received fifty cents for each day worked, and the farmer furnished the meals. Peanuts became the new cash crop, and farming held this distressed community together.

Although the guns ceased to fire at Appomattox Court House, the harsh treatment of the South by the North continued under the Radical

Republicans in the Congress and the administration of the Reconstruction Era and military occupation of the South. The state of Virginia was not admitted into the Union until 1870.

Railroad depot buildings are the focal point of this photograph. The circular Sibley tents and smaller wall tents were likely occupied by Construction Corps employees. Captain Elisha E. Camp, an assistant quartermaster, was in charge of the supply depot. He and other assistant quartermasters were under the command of Brigadier General Rufus Ingalls. Stilts and planking for Captain Camp's quartermaster wharf, the largest of the eight wharves, are seen beyond the buildings.

Virginia Tech Imagebase

Appomattox Manor was occupied by Brigadier General Rufus Ingalls, the chief quartermaster on Grant's staff. With the help of his many assistants, Ingalls provided transportation and housing for the men and animals. The Quartermaster General's Department also issued uniforms and all equipment except ordnance and food. Mathew Brady took this photograph of Ingalls and an unknown group of friends in the spring of 1865.

LC

Building storehouse and railroad depot at City Point, Virginia.

LC

Transports unloaded their supplies directly onto the rail cars that then distributed them around Grant's lines.

LC

The supply wagons reached destinations that were inaccessible by railroad.

LC

Barrels of supplies at City Point are stacked four deep on the commissary wharf to meet the staggering amount of supplies needed by the army. Each day the animals—horses, mules, and cattle—consumed 600 tons of grain and hay. A twenty-day supply of forage was kept on hand for the animals. Warehouses held thirty days' rations in addition to the clothing, shoes, camp equipment, and other items needed to maintain 100,000 Union soldiers.

LC

The U.S. Military Railroad Construction Corps moved into City Point only three days after Grant's arrival and the Union army's initial attack on the Confederate line at Petersburg. Two to three thousand Construction Corps workers quartered throughout the area. The quartermaster repair depot employed an additional 1,600 carpenters, blacksmiths, and laborers. Eight large barracks stood on the north side of Pierce Street, just above the intersection of Pierce and Water streets.

LC

Immediately upon their arrival, the Construction Corps began building the warehouses, wharves, and railroad needed for supplies and war materials and repaired the City Point Railroad, built in 1838. City Point now linked the military supply depot with soldiers on the front lines. As the Army of the Potomac extended its line around Petersburg, the railroad kept up by extending track from a branch off the City Point Line. By the end of the ten-month siege almost twenty-two miles of track had been laid.

LC

The resplendent Zouave 114th Pennsylvania Regiment, detailed as provost guard and garrison troops, pose in August 1864.

LC

One of the unchanging rules of war is that men die. The U.S. Sanitary Commission began a cemetery near the depot hospital. After the war the U.S. Burial Corps reinterred widely scattered bodies in national cemeteries. Now operated by the Veterans Administration, City Point National Cemetery has 6,763 Civil War burials. Of this number, 1,423 are unknown, 5,238 are Union, and 102 are Confederate soldiers. The cemetery is on land that once belonged to Cawsons, the birthplace of John Randolph of Roanoke.

LC

A row of 12-pounders and their carriages, awaiting transportation to the front.

LC

Maintaining the enormous City Point supply base required hundreds of special laborers who required special encampment. Their winter quarters outside the base kept them close to their unending work.

LC

Part 3

Capture of Lieutenant General Ulysses S. Grant

On August 9, 1864, while General Grant was sitting in front of his tent talking to General G. H. Sharpe, his assistant provost marshal told him there might be spies in the area. At that time, an ammunition barge moored near a wharf exploded, throwing live ammunition, hardware, and fragments all over the area where people and tents were located. Forty-three people were killed and 126 were wounded. It was assumed that Rebel secret service agents had planted the explosive device. Grant narrowly escaped violent death.

After the war ended, it was found that John Maxwell, an agent of the Confederate secret service, had gotten powder planted in the barge and set off the explosion. City Point would make a good target for sabotage or attack, and this was not overlooked by the Confederate military and secret service.

In early September 1864 a Confederate naval officer posing as a Baltimore salvage and iron buyer made his way through the depot to see how and where an attack could be made to damage or destroy the spread-out and extensive operations of the base. Pretending to be interested in buying supplies or damaged materials or articles, the secret agent talked with military personnel and employees, all the while finding out the lay of the land. His name was Ralph Jamison of Norfolk, Virginia. After several days of surveillance he made a map of the installation and went to see Secret Service Agent George Peyton. Together they looked at the map to determine the most vulnerable place to stage a military attack. They then went to see the nearest commander of Southern troops in the area, Colonel Richard L. T. Beale of the 10th Virginia Cavalry, whose troops were within striking distance of the City Point railroad leading to Petersburg.

After review and discussion of the project, Colonel Beale took the agents to see General William H. F. Lee, his division commander. The general reviewed the matter and decided that he would send two of his regiments to make a frontal attack if supported at the same time by a naval disruptive action along the wharves and railroad adjacent to the river. Jamison and Peyton were pleased and told the general that they would contact the navy and obtain its support of the operation and proposed arrangements for putting the plan into action. The two men met with the naval commander of the James River Squadron, Roger Wright, along with Major John E. Taylor of General Lee's staff, and developed a plan for a unified assault to be made exactly at 1 a.m., October 2.

The plan called for:

1. Three small watercraft loaded with sailors. Fire bombs and guns were to enter the harbor and attack cargo ships, equipment, warehouses, and wharves.
2. Selected men from various companies were to attack and capture General Grant and no more than two members of his staff.
3. Other troops were to overcome the defending garrison and fire equipment and warehouses.

The troops were to retire when the mission was accomplished and at the order of Colonel R. L. T. Beale. To be more easily identifiable in the dark, every trooper was to wrap a white cloth around his left arm. Troops were told to carry items that could serve as torches. No one was to be told of the plan until the day of operations. It was known that the depot was protected by the Zouave 114th Pennsylvania Volunteers as provost guard and garrison troops, and stout resistance had to be overcome.

General Lee approved the plan and steps were taken to determine the route to be followed to and from the base and the preparation of the naval boats.

Early on October 1, Colonel Beale called his troops together and told them to prepare for a night assault but did not disclose the specific location. That evening, with a local guide directing the advance, the troopers went east and south of City Point through woods and brush below the Union picket lines to a seldom used trail leading to the depot area.

Following this trail at the appropriate time, the colonel led his men to arrive at the depot at the appointed hour. When that time came, the troopers charged through the picket lines to the base complex. Arriving in the area, they encountered the defending force.

The special troopers assigned to capture General U. S. Grant headed directly for the cabins in the living quarters area. The rest of the troopers were shooting and attacking the defenders and setting the warehouses, equipment, wagons, hay, and other supplies on fire. Meanwhile the sailors in the wharf area had dropped fire bombs into a cargo ship to set it on fire and threw fire bombs in a pile of hay, which in turn burned the warehouse.

People came running out of the cabins to see what was going on. They were immediately confronted by the armed troopers and were forced to surrender or try to escape and get shot. The outnumbered garrison and guards were unable to stop the troopers' raid on the buildings and supplies in the area.

After a lengthy period of time, the invaders, along with their captives, retired down the road near the City Point railroad to the Petersburg area.

Generals Grant, Sharpe, and John A. Rawlins were the only captives. They emerged from their quarters to face the troopers at gunpoint.

There were casualties. Six troopers were killed, ten wounded, and three missing. The wounded were left at the hospital where the wounded garrison troops were taken. Federal casualties were unknown. Two sailors escaped and three were wounded and taken to the hospital and three were missing.

After General W. H. F. Lee notified the War Department in Richmond of the capture of Grant, Sharpe, and Rawlins, he received a telegram from Secretary of War James Seddon ordering him to bring the captives to his office. In the meantime, Secretary of War Seddon and General Samuel Cooper, the adjutant general, met with President Jefferson Davis to discuss the capture and its ramification.

It was a delicate matter. The Richmond newspapers had found out about the capture, and large, bold headlines and details of the raid and capture stirred the emotions of people both north and south. The question now was what to do with the captives and whatever action decided upon would cause the greatest uproar. General Cooper brought up the fact that there was a deplorable manpower shortage in the army and suggested that in exchange for the officers, the Federal army release all Confederate prisoners of war from their fourteen prisoner of war camps. He pointed out that the Union armies had about twice as many troops as the South.

His proposal would return perhaps 40,000 to 50,000 men to their military units. This sounded fairly reasonable. While this condition for release of the captives was being discussed, a telegram from United States Secretary of War Edwin M. Stanton to Secretary James Seddon demanded the immediate release and return of General Grant and his officers to his army.

Members of both the Confederate and U.S. Congress and the media were involved in heated discussions on what action should be taken by President Davis. After several days, the captured officers were brought to Richmond and placed in a private home under well-guarded conditions.

After several more days of deliberation, it was thought that General Grant's officers might be released, but that Grant would not leave until all Confederate prisoners of war were shipped to prisoner of war holding stations and from there returned to their respective military units. This solution and position was presented to Secretary of War Stanton, who was furious when he read the message.

Was Grant worth 40,000 to 50,000 Rebel troops? There was but one answer. Return General Grant! But not until the release and return of the Confederate prisoners of war was completed. Secretary Stanton talked to President Lincoln, who, reluctantly, agreed to President Davis's demand since he had no other choice but to get his commander in chief back in the saddle. A telegram from Seddon to Stanton confirmed the approval of the release of Generals Rawlins and Sharpe and requested details for arranging the release of the prisoners of war. When Grant met Rawlins the last time before his fellow captives' release, Grant gave him orders that he wanted transmitted to his field commanders. He also told Rawlins, his adjutant, to send a personal telegram to Secretary of War Stanton, suggesting that he appoint Major General William T. Sherman acting commander in chief until he could return to duty.

The receiving stations for the prisoners of war are listed below. The U.S. Army was to send the Confederate prisoners to these stations as indicated and arrange for their transportation to the nearest location of their known field command.

Receiving Stations for Prisoners of War

POW Camp	*Receiving Station*
Camp Chase	Columbus, Ohio
Camp Morton	Indianapolis, Indiana

David's Island	New York City
Fort Columbus	New York City
Fort Delaware	Wilmington, Delaware
Fort McHenry	Baltimore, Maryland
Fort Monroe	Norfolk, Virginia
Fort Warren	Boston, Massachusetts
Johnson's Island	Toledo, Ohio
Newport News	Newport News, Virginia
Old Capitol	Washington, D.C.
Point Lookout	Washington, D.C.
Rock Island	Chicago, Illinois
Wheeling	Wheeling, West Virginia

Releases were to be made within sixty days. Release of General Grant was to be effective upon completion of inspections and approval of the Confederate army provost marshal. These instructions were forwarded to Secretary of War Stanton for action. The secretary followed through and the camps were emptied and inspections completed within sixty days. General Grant was released on February 25, 1865, and the Southern armies struggled on briefly with a few more worn-out, hungry, ill-equipped, ragged, dejected but valiant men at arms.

The operation of the mammoth City Point military supply base was, in large measure, responsible for the success of the well-equipped and supplied Federal armies. And what happened to Colonel R. L. T. Beale? He was promoted to brigadier general on January 6, 1865.

After the last drumbeat at Appomattox Court House sounded, the surly Federal Secretary of War Edwin Stanton and radical Republican leaders in Congress wanted to bring President Jefferson Davis and other Southern leaders to trial. Supreme Court Chief Justice Salmon P. Chase wrote to Stanton and told him that by the Constitution secession was not rebellion and that Davis and his leaders could not be convicted of treason. Moreover, President Andrew Johnson and Stanton proposed the arrest of all Confederate colonels and generals. General Grant, to his credit, stated that "You will have to whip me and my army before one hair on one head of the men whom we captured, and to whom we promised protection, shall perish."

When Grant chose to attach his headquarters to the Army of the Potomac, his movements depended on the army's movements. The siege of Petersburg intensified as the summer of 1864 turned into autumn. In November, Grant, his staff, and the soldiers substituted log cabins for cloth tents. Grant's two-room cabin was shaped like the letter T, with the front room serving as an office while his sleeping quarters occupied the back room. The cabin appears on the left in the photograph. The East Wing of Appomattox Manor is in the background. Major General John A. Rawlins, chief of staff, occupied an identical cabin to the right of Grant's. The cabins provided a clear view of the confluence of the James and Appomattox rivers.

LC

Rear view of General Ulysses S. Grant's headquarters.

LC

On August 9, 1864, Confederate saboteurs set off an explosion at City Point that rocked the ordnance wharves.

LC

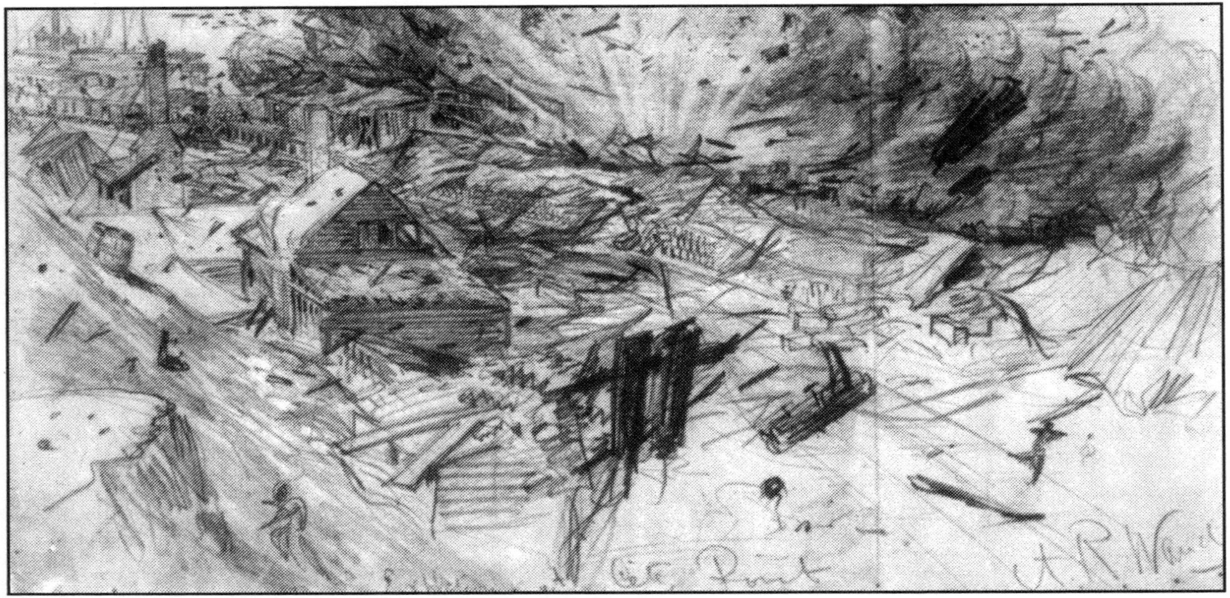

Explosion at City Point. **A pencil drawing by Alfred R. Waud.**

LC

The many masts and lines of guns and caissons show the ceaseless activity that continued around the clock.

LC

The extensive wharves and warehouses were the focal point of quartermaster activity, providing transportation, clothing, camp equipment, fuel, forage, and equipment repair. Each day an average of seventy-five sailing vessels, forty steamboats, and one hundred barges brought in supplies and materials from Northern ports. In one instance, a fleet of ninety vessels arrived carrying twenty-four locomotives and 275 boxcars.

LC

A more sophisticated telegraphic operation was soon established, employing more than a dozen key operators, shown here in their summer quarters.

LC

About the Author

Following many years of distinguished service in the United States Air Force, which included a short time of duty in The White House, Colonel Walbrook D. Swank has added this unique book to the twenty-two he has already written or edited.

He is the recipient of the prestigious National Henry Timrod Southern Culture Award, the Sir Moses Ezekiel Award for Achievement in the Arts and Literature, numerous major Department of the Air Force awards for outstanding and meritorious service, and a distinguished service citation from the Secretary of the Treasury.

The colonel has received letters of commendation from former U.S. Senator George Allen of Virginia, former Virginia Governor Mark Warner, and the Senate of Virginia for his outstanding contributions to historic preservation and our Southern heritage.

The author's grandfather, Thomas S. Davis, and his younger brother, John N. Davis, were members of Company I, 10th Virginia Cavalry in Major General W. H. F. Lee's Cavalry Division. Thomas was wounded in 1864, and in 1865 John was taken prisoner by Union troops and sent to Libby Prison in Richmond, Virginia. They were relatives of President Jefferson Davis and are the subject of a book by the author entitled *Clash of the Sabres: Blue and Gray*.

— ALSO BY THE AUTHOR —

Defending the Southern Confederacy

The Men in Gray

Reverend Robert Catlett Cave wrote *The Men In Gray* in 1911 to help explain the Southern viewpoint on the conflict. At the unveiling of the monument to the Confederate sailors & soldiers of the Southern Confederacy in Libby Park, Richmond, Virginia, his oration sparked a controversy that led to the writing and explanation contained in this book.

ISBN 978-1-57249-261-5 • PB $15.95

Stonewall Jackson's Foot Cavalry

Company A, 13th Virginia Infantry

In the early days of the war there were approximately 1,540 men in the 10 companies of the 13th Virginia Infantry Regiment. As the war progressed, attrition severely reduced the ranks, and at the surrender at Appomattox only 63 men were present. Company A, with an initial strength of 166, had remaining only 22 men at Appomattox, one of whom was Private George Q. Peyton. His regiment, known as the Montpelier Guard, was a part of General "Stonewall" Jackson's famous "Foot Cavalry."

ISBN 978-1-57249-211-0 • PB $19.95

A Treasury of Confederate Heritage

A Panorama of Life in the South

The character of the men in gray is reflected in the everyday life and sayings of a society that present a more intimate knowledge of them. Four years of heroic sacrifice, glory, suffering, fortitude, and valor are interwoven in this outstanding anthology about the South and its culture. The wit and humor, the quaint sayings, and rough camp jests and pranks that prevailed in the ranks of the armed forces are included as well. The collection includes 245 stories about battlefield, camp and hospital incidents, guerilla exploits, home life in Dixie, and action on the high seas.

ISBN 978-1-57249-351-3 • PB $24.95

WHITE MANE PUBLISHING CO., INC.

To Request a Catalog Please Write to:

WHITE MANE PUBLISHING COMPANY, INC.

P.O. Box 708 • Shippensburg, PA 17257

e-mail: marketing@whitemane.com

CPSIA information can be obtained
at www.ICGtesting.com
Printed in the USA
BVHW04s1735110918
527178BV00010B/65/P

9 781572 493964